Collars
for Kids

LEISURE ARTS, INC. • Maumelle, Arkansas

ISBN-13/EAN: 978-1-4647-1682-9

Meet Cony Larsen

Cony Larsen of Highland, Utah, is a designer and author of crochet books and tools. Describing her style as Boho Chic with a touch of traditional, Cony says she loves projects that can be finished in a day or two, and finds inspiration in the children in her life, her garden, and her love of hand-loomed textiles and fibers. For more about her designs, tools, and aid programs for her Guatemalan homeland, visit her website, conylarsenbooks.com.

Look for the camera
in our instructions & watch our technique videos made just for you!
@ www.leisurearts.com/6379

Contents

Collar with White Pansies

■□□□ BEGINNER

Finished Size: 2¼" height x 13½" circumference (5.5 cm x 34.5 cm)

SHOPPING LIST

Yarn (Fine Weight) **SUPER FINE 1**
[1.75 ounces, 437 yards
(50 grams, 400 meters) per ball]:
☐ 1 ball (for Collar only)

Thread (Bedspread Weight) **LACE 0**
[1.75 ounces, 284 yards
(50 grams, 260 meters) per ball]:
☐ 1 ball (for Pansies only)

Crochet Hooks
☐ Size C (2.75 mm) **and**
☐ Steel, Size 4 (1.75 mm)
or sizes needed for gauge

Additional Supplies
☐ Yarn needle
☐ ⁵⁄₈" (16 mm) Ribbon -
1 yard (1 meter)
☐ Rhinestones, optional
☐ Rhinestone setter, optional
☐ ½" (12 mm) Buttons - 2

GAUGE INFORMATION

6 sts = 1" (2.5 cm)/ 7 rows = 1" (2.5 cm)
Gauge Swatch: Crochet a 12 ch 8 rows square swatch of scs to check your tension. Correct your tension if necessary to make sure you have the right gauge before you get started; you can change hook size or yarn weight to correct your tension and achieve the right gauge.

Collar Section
Ch 81.

Row 1: Sc in each ch, ch 1, turn (80 sts).

Row 2: Sc in each sc, ch 1, turn (80 sts).

Row 3: Sc in next 14 sc, 2 sc in next sc *sc in next 9 sc, 2 sc in next sc; rep from * 5 times, sc in last 15 sc, ch 1, turn, (86 sts).

Row 4: Rep Row 2, (86 sts).

Row 5: Sc in next 15 sc, 2 sc in next sc *sc in next 10 sc, 2 sc in next sc; rep from * 5 times, sc in last 15 sc, ch 1, turn, (92 sts).

Row 6: Rep Row 2, (92 sts).

Row 7: Sc in next 15 sc, 2 sc in next sc *sc in next 11 sc, 2 sc in next sc; rep from * 5 times, sc in last 16 sc, ch 1, turn, (98 sts).

Row 8: Rep Row 2, (98 sts).

Row 9: Sc in next 16 sc, 2 sc in next sc *sc in next 12 sc, 2 sc in next sc; rep from * 5 times, sc in last 16 sc, ch 1, turn, (104 sts).

Row 10: Rep Row 2, (104 sts).

Row 11: Sc in next 16 sc, 2 sc in next sc *sc in next 13 sc, 2 sc in next sc; rep from * 5 times, sc in last 17 sc, ch 1, turn, (110 sts).

Rows 12-13: Rep Row 2, ch 1, turn (110 sts).

Edging

Work all edging sts in front loops only.

Row 1: Sc in 1st sc, *sk 1 sc, 5 dc Shell in  front loop only of next sc, sk next sc, sl st in next sc; rep from * across, sc in last st, ch 1, turn collar.

Row 2: Ch 1, sc in front loop of 1st sc, *5 dc Shell in **front loop only** in same sc as previous row Shell, sk next sc, sl st in same sc as previous row, sk next sc; rep from * across, end 5 dc Shell in same sc as previous row, sk next sc, sc in last sc. Fasten off. Weave in ends. Block (page 44).

Pansies (make 12)

With Steel hook 4/1.75mm and thread, make a Magic Ring (see page 47).

Rnd 1: *Ch 2, 3 dc, hdc, 3 dc, ch 3, sl st in ring; rep from * 3 times to make a three petal Pansy. Fasten off leaving a 6" (15 cm) tail to attach Pansy to collar. Block (see page 44).

Finishing

Attach each flower to the collar, making sure to space flowers evenly across the length of the collar, secure each flower to the collar with yarn needle using 6" (15 cm) tail; attach a rhinestone to the center of each flower or make a Bullion Stitch (see page 39) in the center of each flower.

Ribbon ties, cut two pieces of ribbon 18" (45.5 cm) long; sew ribbon to each end of collar. Sew buttons at each corner, see picture below.

Collar on a Ribbon

● □ □ □ **BEGINNER**

Finished Size: 13" circumference x 3" height (33 cm x 7.5 cm)

SHOPPING LIST

Yarn (Light Weight)
[1.75 ounces, 126 yards
(50 grams, 115 meters) per ball]:
☐ 1 ball

Crochet Hook
☐ Size B (2.25 mm)
or sizes needed for gauge

Additional Supplies
☐ ¼" (7 mm) Ribbon - 1 yard
(1 meter)
☐ Fabric pen
☐ Sewing needle
☐ Matching thread

GAUGE INFORMATION

6 sts = 1" (2.5 cm)/ 6 rows = 1" (2.5 cm)

Gauge Swatch: Crochet a 12 ch 8 rows square swatch of scs to check your tension. Correct your tension if necessary to make sure you have the right gauge before you get started; you can change hook size or yarn weight to correct your tension and achieve the right gauge.

Collar

Fold ribbon in half and mark center with a fabric pen; measure 5½" (14 cm) from the center to the right, that's where you will start your first sc, 🎥 tie yarn with a knot at the 5½" (14 cm) point (see photo below), ch 1.

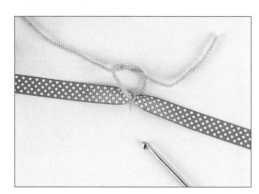

Row 1: 104 Sc around ribbon, make sure to space scs evenly on ribbon, ch 1, turn, (104 sts).

Row 2: Sc in each sc across, ch 1, turn, (104 sts).

Row 3: Sc in 1st sc, *ch 2, sk next sc, sl st in next sc; rep from * across, sc in last sc, ch 1, turn.

Row 4: Sc in 1st sc, ch 3, sl st in 1st ch-2 space, *ch 3, sl st in next ch-2 space; rep from * across, ch 3, sc in last sc, ch 1, turn.

Row 5: Sc in 1st sc, ch 4, sl st in 1st ch-3 space, *ch 4, sl st in next ch-3 space; rep from * across, ch 4, sc in last sc, ch 1, turn.

Row 6: Sc in 1st sc, ch 3, sl st in 1st ch-4 space, *ch 4, sl st in next ch-4 space; rep from * across, ch 3, sc in last sc, ch 1, turn.

Row 7: Sc in 1st sc, ch 4, sl st in 1st ch-4 space, *ch 4, sl st in next ch-4 space; rep from * across, ch 4, sc in last sc, ch 1, turn.

Row 8: Sc in 1st sc, ch 3, sl st in 1st ch-4 space, *ch 4, sl st in next ch-4 space; rep from * across, ch 3, sc in last sc, ch 1, turn.

Row 9: Rep Row 7, ch 1, turn.

Row 10: Sc in 1st sc, ch 4, sl st in 1st ch-4 space, *ch 5, sl st in next ch-4 space; rep from * across, ch 5, sc in last sc, ch 1, turn.

Row 11: Sc in 1st sc, ch 4, sl st in 1st ch-5 space, *ch 5, sl st in next ch-5 space; rep from * across, ch 4, sc in last sc, ch 1, turn.

Finishing

Thread sewing needle, secure the first and last sc to the ribbon with a few stitches. Cut ribbon ends to desired length for bow.

Block (see page 44).

Look for the camera
in our instructions & watch our
technique videos made just for you!
@ www.leisurearts.com/6379

Gold on a Chain

□□□□ INTERMEDIATE

Finished Size: 2³/₈" height x 13½" circumference (6 cm x 34.5 cm)

Sample A shown on page 14

SHOPPING LIST

Yarn (Medium Weight) **MEDIUM 4**
[3.5 ounces, 280 yards
(100 grams, 256 meters) per ball]:
☐ 1 ball

Crochet Hooks
☐ Size C (2.75 mm)
or size needed for gauge
☐ Steel, Size 4 (1.75 mm)

Additional Supplies
☐ Black/Silver metal chain,
¼" (7 mm) long links,
20¼" (51.5 cm) long (92 links)
☐ Yarn needle

Sample B

SHOPPING LIST

Yarn (Fine Weight) **FINE 2**
[.35 ounces, 28 yards
(10 grams, 26 meters) per ball]:
☐ Color A - 1 ball
☐ Color B - 1 ball

Crochet Hooks
☐ Size C (2.75 mm)
or size needed for gauge
☐ Steel, Size 4 (1.75 mm)

Additional Supplies
Black/Silver metal chain,
¼" (7 mm) long links,
☐ 20¼" (51.5 cm) long (92 links)
☐ Yarn needle
☐ Small swivel lobster clasp

GAUGE INFORMATION

6 sts = 1" (2.5 cm)/ 6 rows = 1" (2.5 cm)

Gauge Swatch: Crochet a 12 ch 8 rows square swatch of scs to check your tension. Correct your tension if necessary to make sure you have the right gauge before you get started; you can change hook size or yarn weight to correct your tension and achieve the right gauge.

Collar

Measure 92 links of the chain and cut, about 20¼" (51.5 cm) long chain, skip the first 18 chain links, join color A to 19th link with hook size 4/1.75mm, see photo A.

Photo A

Row 1: Ch 1, sc in same link, *2 sc in next link, sc in next link; rep from * across, end with sc in link 57, you should have 17 links left, ch 1, turn, (85 scs).

Row 2: Sc in each sc across, ch 1, turn.

Switch to hook C/2-2.75mm.

Rows 3-5: Sc in each sc across, ch 1, turn, (85 scs). Drop color A and join color B if working Sample B.

Row 6: *Sc in next 3 scs, 2 sc in next sc; rep from * across, sc in last 4 scs, ch 1, turn, (105 scs).

Rows 7-8: Sc in each sc across, ch 1, turn, (105 scs).

Row 9: *Sc in next 7 scs, 2 sc in next sc; rep from * across, sc in last sc, ch 1, turn, (118 scs).

Rows 10-13: Sc in each sc across, ch 1, turn, (118 scs).

If you are working with thinner yarn, like our sample B, work the following rows:

Fasten off color B and join color A to last row.

Rows 14-16: Sc in each sc across, ch 1, turn, (118 scs).

Edging

Row 1: Sc in 1st sc, *ch 4, sk 2 sc, sl st in next sc; rep from * across, sc in last sc. Fasten off. Weave in ends.

Finishing

See page 45 for Tassel instructions.

For Sample B, attach the small lobster clasp to inside corner links of collar. Attach a tassel on each side with needle and thread. Block (see page 44).

Wasabi with Pink Edge

●□□□ **BEGINNER**

Finished Size: 2½" height x 8" length (6.5 cm x 20.5 cm), this collar is made in 2 halves.

SHOPPING LIST

Yarn

(Super Fine Weight Cotton)
[1.52 ounces, 150 yards
(43 grams, 137 meters) per ball]:
☐ Color A (Green) - 1 ball

SUPER FINE 1

Thread (Size 5)

[.125 ounces, 27 yards (5 grams,
25 meters) per ball]:
☐ Color B (White) - 1 ball
☐ Color C (Pink) - 2 balls

Crochet Hooks

☐ Size C (2.75 mm) **and**
☐ Steel, size 4 (1.75 mm)
  (for edging)
  or sizes needed for gauge

Additional Supplies

☐ ⁵/₈" (16 mm) Ribbon - 1 yard
  (1 meter)
☐ Yarn needle
☐ Sewing needle
☐ Matching thread
☐ ⁵/₈" (16 mm) Button - 2

GAUGE INFORMATION

5 sts = 1" (2.5 cm)/6 rows = 1" (2.5 cm)
Gauge Swatch: Crochet a 12 ch 8 rows
square swatch of scs to check your
tension. Correct your tension if necessary
to make sure you have the right gauge
before you get started; you can change
hook size or yarn weight to correct your
tension and achieve the right gauge.

Collar Section (make 2)

Reverse shaping on 2nd collar half.

Ch 41.

Row 1: Sc in 2nd ch from hook and in
each ch across, ch 1, turn (40 sts).

Row 2: Sc in each st, (ch 1, sc in last
sc), ch 1, turn (41 sts).

Row 3 - Increase row: Sc in 1st 13 sc,
2 sc in next sc, sc in next 13 sc, 2 sc
in next sc, sc in last 13 sc, ch 1, turn
(43 sts).

Row 4: Rep Row 2, (44 sts).

Row 5 - Increase row: Sc in 1st 14 sts,
3 sc in next st, sc in next 14 sts, 3 sc
in next st, sc in next 14 sts; ch 1, turn,
(48 sts).

Row 6: Rep Row 2, ch 1, turn, (49 sts).

Row 7: Sc in each st across, ch 1, turn
(49 sts).

Rows 8-12: Rep Row 2 and 7
alternating (52 sts). Fasten off.
Weave in ends.

Edging

With **right** side of collar facing you and
using hook size 4/1.75mm, join one
strand of color B to top back corner of the
right collar half.

Row 1: Working down side of collar, sc,
ch 1, in each row end st; sc, ch 1, twice in
corner st; sc, ch 1, in each st across bottom
edge; sc, ch 1 twice in corner st; working
up front side of collar, sc, ch 1, in each row
end st; end sc in last row end st.

ow 2: Join two strands of color C with a
st to 1st sc of rnd 1. Sc, ch 1, dc in next
n-1 sp and in each ch-1 sp around collar
dge; sl st in last sc.

peat Edging instructions for second
llar half.

Finishing

Cut two pieces of ribbon each 20" (51 cm)
long. Fold one end by ½" (12 mm), place
on the top back corner of collar and
secure to collar by sewing a button on top
of it. Repeat with other section.

With a yarn needle and color A, join left
and right sections of collar in the front
top corners by sewing a few small
stitches. Make a small bow and pin,
stitch, or hot glue it to the front where
the two sections join.

Shawl Collar & Mini Pom-poms

■■■□ INTERMEDIATE

Finished Size: 2" height x 15" circumference (5 cm x 38 cm)

SHOPPING LIST

Thread (Bedspread Weight) [LACE 0]
[1.75 ounces, 284 yards
(50 grams, 260 meters) per ball]:
- ☐ Color A (White) - 2 balls
- ☐ Color B (Blue) - 2 balls

Crochet Hooks
- ☐ Size B (2.25 mm) **and**
- ☐ Steel, Size 4 (1.75 mm)
  or sizes needed for gauge

Additional Supplies
- ☐ Yarn needle
- ☐ Mini Pom-Poms -
  1 yard (1 meter)
- ☐ Ribbon for bow - 8" (20.5 cm)
- ☐ Small snap
- ☐ ½" (12 mm) Buttons - 2

Collar is worked holding two strands of thread together throughout.

GAUGE INFORMATION

6 sts = 1" (2.5 cm)/6 rows = 1" (2.5 cm)
Gauge Swatch: Crochet a 12 ch 8 rows square swatch of scs to check your tension. Correct your tension if necessary to make sure you have the right gauge before you get started; you can change hook size or yarn weight to correct your tension and achieve the right gauge.

STITCH GUIDE

📹▶ Spike Sc: Insert hook in corresponding st 1 row **below** next st, yo, pull up loop to height of current row, yo, pull through 2 loops on hook.

Collar Section

With two strands of color A Ch 79.

Row 1: Sc in 2nd ch from hook and in each ch across, ch 1, turn, (78 sts).

Row 2: *Sc in next 2 sc, 2 sc in next sc; rep from * across, ch 1, turn, (104 sts).

Rows 3-4: Sc in each sc across, ch 1, turn, (104 sts).

Row 5: *Sc in next 5 sc, 2 sc in next sc; rep from * across, sc in last 2 sc, ch 1, turn, (121 sts).

Row 6: Rep Row 3, drop color A, turn, (121 sts).

Row 7: Join two strands of color B to beg sc, sc in 1st 6 sc, **Spike sc** in next sc from prior row; *sc in next 5 sc, **Spike sc**; rep from * across; end with sc in last 6 sc. Fasten off color B. Weave in ends, do not turn, (121 sts).

Row 8: Pick up two strands of color A, ch 3, dc in 1st sc, *sk next 3 sc, {2 dc, ch 1, 2 dc} in next sc; rep from * across, end sk next 3 sc, 2 dc in last sc, ch 1, turn, (149 sts).

Row 9: Sc in each sc and each ch-1 sp across, ch 1, turn, (149 sts).

Row 10: Sc in each sc across, end with 2 sc in last sc, do **not** fasten off, finish side edge as follows: 2 sc in corner sc, sc in next st, ch 8 to make buttonhole, work 10-11 scs evenly spaced up the side of the collar, ch 8 for top buttonhole, sl st in last corner st. Fasten off. Weave in ends.

Finishing opposite Side Edge
With **right** side facing you, join two strands of color A to corner of beg sc from Row 1, work 12-14 scs evenly spaced down the side of collar, sl st in last st. Fasten off. Weave in ends.

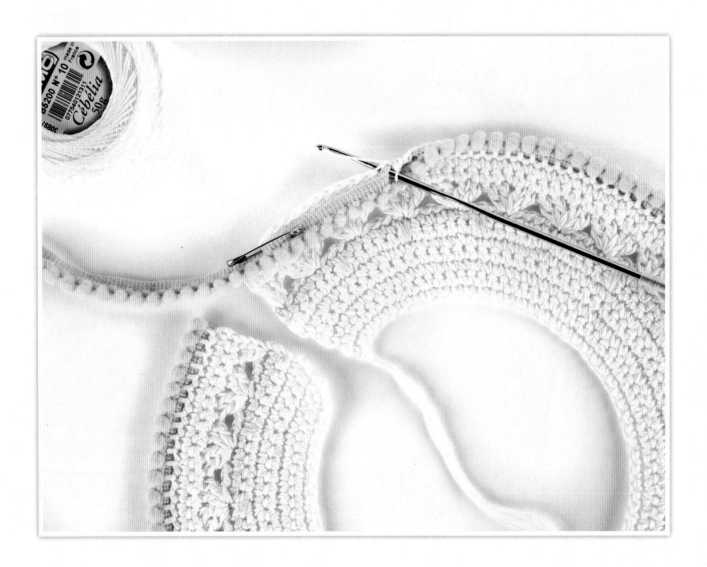

om-pom Edging

easure the bottom edge of collar and
t a piece of the Mini Pom-poms the
me size plus 3" (9 cm). Place right
des together, pin pom-pom beading
collar.

ith crochet hook 4/1.75mm and single
and of cotton thread; 📹 join color A
1st sc, piercing through all thickness.

ow 1: Ch 1, sc, ch 1 in each sc across;
m pom-poms off at the corner. Fasten
f. Weave in ends.

Finishing

Overlap collar ends over each other by
2" (5 cm) and pin in place (collar may
be adjusted to fit a bigger size without
overlapping); mark placement for
buttons, with a yarn needle and cotton
thread, attach two buttons securely. Use
a safety pin to attach bow to front or
sew it on.

Rings Around the Collar

⬛⬜⬜⬜ **BEGINNER**

Finished Size: 13" (33 cm) in circumference.

GAUGE INFORMATION
Gauge is not crucial for this project.

Collar
Crochet around 7 rings using different colors of the cotton yarn.

Rnd 1: 🎥 Join yarn to ring with a knot (see photo below), ch 1, work 50 sc around the ring. Join with sl st to beg sc, (50 scs).

Rnd 2: Ch 1, sc in each sc around. Join with sl st to beg sc, (50 sts).

Rnd 3: Ch 1, sl st in 1st sc, *ch 1, sl st in next sc; rep from * around. Join with sl st to beg ch. Fasten off. Weave in ends.

Finishing
With yarn needle and cream color yarn and back side of rings facing you, starting with first ring, *insert needle at the base of one of the stitches from Rnd 3, pick up second ring and join to first ring with a couple of whipstitches Fasten off.

Skip 16 sc on second ring, insert needl at the base of one of the stitches from Rnd 3, pick up third ring and join to second ring with a couple of whipstitches. Rep from * until you hav joined all seven rings.

Run full length of ribbon through front of end ring, between 2 sts of rnd 2 (16 sc from last attachment), then thread ribbon up through other end ring at corresponding places.

Tassels (Make 2)
Follow instructions on page 45 to make 2 tassels. Attach a tassel to each end ring.

Florets on a Ribbon

◐▢▢▢ **BEGINNER**

Finished Size: 11" (28 cm) long when Florets are nested side by side on the ribbon x 2" (5 cm) height

SHOPPING LIST

Yarn (Medium Weight) **MEDIUM 4**
[3.5 ounces, 200 yards
(100 grams, 183 meters) per ball]:
(We chose 7 different colors, you can
use leftover yarn from your stash.)
☐ 1 ball each

Crochet Hook
☐ Size G (4 mm)
or size needed for gauge

Additional Supplies
Sample A
☐ ¾" (19 mm) Ribbon -
   1½ yards (1.5 meters)
Sample B
☐ 1½" (4 cm) Ribbon -
   1½ yards (1.5 meters)
Both Samples
☐ Fabric pen
☐ Yarn needle
☐ Matching thread
☐ ¼" (7 mm) Brads for center of
   flowers - 9

GAUGE INFORMATION

Gauge is not essential for this project. Just make sure to buy chunky yarn for your flowers so they will be big enough.

Gauge Swatch: Each floret is approximately 5" (12.5 cm) circumference by 2" (5 cm) across.

Florets (make 9)

Make a  Magic Ring (see page 47).

To make a petal, work in ring *ch 3, 6 dtr, join with sl st to top of beg ch 3, ch 3, sl st in ring; rep from * until you have 5 petals, (you may want to make your florets with 6 petals); fasten off after you make the last petal, grab the tail of the Magic Ring and pull firmly to close the ring.

Place a brad through the center of the ring.

Finishing

Fold ribbon in half and mark center; place first floret at center mark, arrang florets very close together (4 florets or each side of center). Use heavy thread and yarn needle to sew each floret to ribbon with a few running stitches (se page 46).

Clip ends of ribbon to desired length diagonally.

African Flower Collar

◼◻◻◻ **BEGINNER**

Finished Size: 2½" height x 13½" circumference (6.5 cm x 34.5 cm).

GAUGE INFORMATION

5 sts = 1" (2.5 cm)/ 6 rows =1" (2.5 cm)
Gauge Swatch: Crochet a 12 ch 8 rows square swatch of scs to check your tension. Correct your tension if necessary to make sure you have the right gauge before you get started; you can change hook size or yarn weight to correct your tension and achieve the right gauge.

STITCH GUIDE

📹 **Spike Sc:** Insert hook in corresponding st 1 row **below** next st, yo, pull up loop to height of current row, yo, pull through 2 loops on hook.

Collar Section

With hook size D/3 (3.25mm) and color A ch 66.

Row 1: Sc in 2nd ch from hook and in each ch across, ch 1, turn, (65 sts, 13½"{34.5 cm}).

Row 2: *Sc in next 2 sc, 2 sc in next sc; rep from * across, end with sc in last 2 sc, ch 1, turn, (86 sts, 15½"{39.5 cm}).

Row 3-5: Sc in each sc across, ch 1, turn, (86 sts, 19¼"{49 cm}).

Row 6: Sc in first 4 sc, 2 sc in next sc, *sc in next 3 sc, 2 sc in next sc; rep from * across, end with sc in last sc, ch 1, turn, (103 sts, 20½"{53 cm}).

Row 7: Rep Row 3, (103 sts).

Switch to hook size C/2 (2.75 mm), ch 3, turn.

Row 8: Dc in 1st sc, sk 2 sc, *(2 dc, ch 1, 2 dc) in next sc, sk 3 sc; rep from * across, end with sk 2 sc, dc in last sc, ch 3, turn, (128 sts).

Row 9: Dc in 1st dc, sk 2 dc, *6 dc in ch-1 space, sk next 4 dc; rep from * across, end with sk next 2 dc, dc in last dc, dc in top of ch 3; ch 1, finish side edge by working 10-11 scs evenly spaced up the side of collar, ch 6 for buttonhole, sl st in last st, (152 sts). Fasten off. Weave in ends.

Finishing opposite Side Edge

With **right** side facing you, join color A to corner of beg sc from Row 1, work 10-11 scs evenly spaced down the side of collar, sl st in last st. Fasten off. Weave in ends.

Edging

With **right** side of collar facing you, join color B in top of ch 3 from Row 9.

Row 1: Sc in same st as join, sc in next dc, **Spike Sc** (see Stitch Guide) between Shells from Row 8, *sc in next 6 dc, **Spike Sc** between Shells from Row 8; rep from * across, end with sc in last 2 sts, (29½" {75 cm} around bottom circumference). Fasten off. Weave in ends.

Finishing

Sew button to back. Embellish front with a bow, pom-poms or charms. Block (see page 44).

Granny Octagon Gems

■□□□ **BEGINNER**

Finished Size: Approximately 13¼" (33.5 cm) at neck edge

SHOPPING LIST

Thread (Size 8)
[.35 ounces, 87 yards (10 grams, 79.5 meters) per ball]:
- ☐ Color A (Pink) - 2 balls
- ☐ Color B (Green) - 2 balls
- ☐ Color C (Orange) - 2 balls
- ☐ Color D (Brown) - 2 balls

Steel Crochet Hook
- ☐ Size 4 (1.75 mm)
  or sizes needed for gauge

Additional Supplies
- ☐ ¼" (7 mm) Ribbon - 1 yard (1 meter)
- ☐ Yarn needle

ch Granny Octagon Gem is worked lding 2 strands of thread together roughout.

AUGE INFORMATION

sts = 1" (2.5 cm) Each Granny Octagon m should measure 2½" (6.25 cm) ameter.

auge Swatch: Crochet a 12 ch 8 rows uare swatch of scs to check your nsion. Correct your tension if necessary make sure you have the right gauge fore you get started; you can change ok size or yarn weight to correct your nsion and achieve the right gauge.

31

STITCH GUIDE

To make a Puff, (6 dc in designated st, join with sl st to beg dc) Puff made.

Granny Octagon Gem
(make 7)

Make a 🎥 Magic Ring (see page 47) with color A.

Rnd 1: Ch 3, *Puff in ring, ch 4; rep from * 4 times. Join with sl st to beg ch-4 space, (4 puffs). Fasten off.

Rnd 2: Join color B to any ch-4 space, ch 3, *Puff in ch-4 space, ch 4, Puff in center of next Puff; rep from * 4 times. Join with sl st to beg ch-4 space, (8 puffs). Fasten off.

Rnd 3: Join color C to any ch-4 space, ch 3, *7 dc in ch-4 space, ch 1; rep from * 8 times. Join with sl st to beg dc, (8 sections of 7 dcs each). Fasten off.

Rnd 4: Join color D to any ch-1 space, ch 1, sc in each st and in each sc and ch-1 space around. Join with sl st to beg sc, (64 sts). Fasten off.

Joining Granny Octagons

Thread yarn needle with color D. Join two octagons as follows:

Place **right** sides of two octagons together, matching up sections, join with 🎥 whip stitching through both layers of a 7 sc section. Fasten off. *Skip two sections, join another octagon to the next section; rep from * until you have joined all octagons.

Neck Edging

Join color D to 1st octagon, two section. prior to the first seam.

Row 1: Ch 1, sl st in next 13 sts, *sk 3 sts 3 dc between octagons, sk 3 sts, sl st in next 9 sts; rep from * across to last octagon, end with sl st in next 13 sts. Fasten off. Weave in ends.

Finishing

Cut ribbon in half; attach one ribbon with a knot between a ch-1 space. Attac second ribbon to opposite side.

Block (see page 44).

Accordion Collar with Pom-poms

 **BEGINNER**

Finished Size: 3" height x 28" length (7.5 cm x 71 cm)

SHOPPING LIST

Yarn (Light Weight) **[LIGHT 3]**
[3.5 ounces, 221 yards
(100 grams, 202 meters) per ball]:
☐ MC - 1 ball
☐ CC - (Gold, Blue and Cream)
   small amount for pom-poms

Crochet Hook
☐ Size E (3.5 mm)
   or size needed for gauge

GAUGE INFORMATION
5 sts = 1" (2.5 cm)/5 rows = 1" (2.5 cm)

Gauge Swatch: Crochet a 12 ch 8 rows square swatch of scs to check your tension. Correct your tension if necessary to make sure you have the right gauge before you get started; you can change hook size or yarn weight to correct your tension and achieve the right gauge.

COLLAR
Ch 15.

Row 1: Sc in 2nd ch from hook and in each ch across, ch 1, turn (14 sts).

Row 2: Sc in 1st sc, ch 1, sk next sc, sc in back loop only of next 12 sc, ch 1, turn (14 sts).

Row 3: Sc in **back loop only** of next 12 sc, ch 1, sk next st, sc in last sc, ch 1, turn (14 sts).

Row 4-144: Rep Row 2 and 3 alternating, (14 sts).

Row 145: Sl st in each st. Fasten off. Weave in ends.

Tie
Ch 200. Fasten off.

Finishing
Weave tie through the ch-1 spaces. Make three 1½" (4 cm) pompoms (see page 46), and attach to the center front of collar.

Look for the camera
in our instructions & watch our technique videos made just for you!
@ www.leisurearts.com/6379

Pink & Gray Florets

○■□□□ **BEGINNER**

Finished Size: 2¼" height x 14½" circumference (5.5 cmx 37 cm)

SHOPPING LIST

Yarn (Light Weight Cotton) [LIGHT 3]
[1.75 ounces, 292 yards
(50 grams, 267 meters) per ball]:
☐ 1 ball (for Collar only)

Thread (Size 5)
[.125 ounces, 27 yards (5 grams,
25 meters) per skein]:
☐ 2 skeins **each** of gray, aqua,
dark gray, green, and gold (for
Florets and Leaves only)

Crochet Hooks
☐ Size D (3.25 mm) **and**
☐ Steel, Size 4 (1.75 mm)
or sizes needed for gauge

Additional Supplies
☐ Yarn needle

Florets are worked holding two strands of thread together throughout.

GAUGE INFORMATION
5½ sts = 1" (2.5 cm) /6 rows = 1" (2.5 cm)
Gauge Swatch: Crochet a 12 ch 8 rows square swatch of scs to check your tension. Correct your tension if necessary to make sure you have the right gauge before you get started; you can change hook size or yarn weight to correct your tension and achieve the right gauge.

Collar Section
Ch 82 with hook D/3-3.25.

Row 1: Sc in each ch, ch 1, turn (81 sts).

Row 2: Sc in next 15 sc, 2 sc in next sc *sc in next 9 sc, 2 sc in sc; rep from * 4 **more** times, sc in last 15 sc, ch 1, turn, (87 sts).

Row 3: Sk 1st sc, sc in each sc across to last 2 sc, sc2tog in last 2 sc, ch 1, turn, (85 sts).

Row 4: Sk 1st sc, sc in next 13 sc, 2 sc in next sc *sc in next 10 sc, 2 sc in sc; rep from * 4 **more** times, sc in last 2 sc, sc2tog in last 2 sc, ch 1, turn, (89 sts).

Row 5: Rep Row 3, ch 1, turn, (87 sts).

Row 6: Sk 1st sc, sc in next 11 sc, 2 sc in next sc *sc in next 11 sc, 2 sc in sc; rep from * 4 **more** times, sc in last 2 sc, sc2tog in last 2 sc, ch 1, turn, (91 sts).

Row 7: Rep Row 3, ch 1, turn, (89 sts).

Row 8: Sk 1st sc, sc in next 10 sc, 2 sc in next sc *sc in next 12 sc, 2 sc in sc; rep from * 4 **more** times, sc in last 2 sc, sc2tog in last 2 sc, ch 1, turn, (93 sts).

Row 9: Rep Row 3, ch 1, turn, (91 sts).

Row 10: Sk 1st sc, sc in next 9 sc, 2 sc in next sc *sc in next 13 sc, 2 sc in sc; rep from * 4 **more** times, sc in last 2 sc, sc2tog in last 2 sc, (95 sts).

Continue to work around edge of collar as follows:
Ch 1, 2 sc in corner st, sc evenly spaced down the side of collar; 3 sc in top corner st, sc across neck line, 3 sc in corner st, sc evenly spaced down the side. Join to beg sc with sl st. Fasten off Weave in ends.

Edging

You will be creating the ties at the same time as you work edging around lower edge of collar.

Ch 50 for first tie, insert the hook in 1st sc at the left top corner of collar, pull yarn through, sl st in same st, *ch 3, sk sc, sl st in next sc; rep from * across to last sc on opposite corner of collar, ch 50 for second tie. Fasten off.

Florets

(make 7 gray, 4 dark gray, 2 gold, and 1 aqua for back motif)

With two strands of color gray and Steel hook 4/1.75 mm, make a 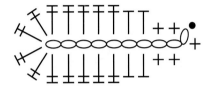 Magic Ring (see page 47).

Rnd 1: *Ch 2, 3 dc, sl st in ring; rep 4 times to make a four petal floret, or three times to make a three petal floret. Fasten off. Weave in ends.

Leaves

(make 2 of each green and gold, and 2 aqua for back motif)

With two strands of color green and Steel hook 4/1.75 mm, ch 10.

Rnd 1: Sc in 2nd ch from hook, sc in next ch, hdc in next 2 ch, dc in next 4 ch, 6 dc in last ch, work on the other side of the ch, dc in next 4 ch, hdc in next 2 ch, sc in next ch, 2 sc in last ch, join with sl st to beg sc. Fasten off. Weave in ends.

Finishing

With yarn needle and gray thread, secure each flower to the collar with running stitch (see page 46); make a bullion stitch in the center of each flower.

Small Leaf ch 10

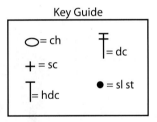

Key Guide

◯ = ch	┬ = dc
+ = sc	
┬ = hdc	● = sl st

☀ How to Make a Bullion Stitch

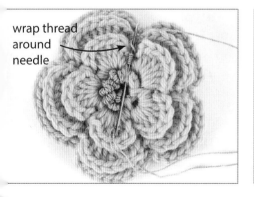

wrap thread around needle

pull needle through

1 Make a ¹/₈" (3 mm) long stitch without pulling needle all the way out, wrap thread around needle 12-15 times, hold wrapped thread in place with your left thumb pressing lightly...

2 Pull needle through all wrapped thread on needle, holding the stitch softly until all thread has passed through the center of wrapped loops...

3 To close the knot, insert the needle back in and bring out just about ¹/₈" (3 mm) back to the beginning of knot, pull thread lightly to secure in place. Repeat steps 1-3 to make more bullion stitches.

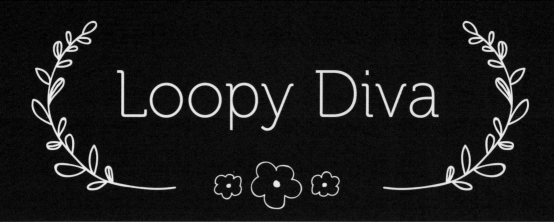

Loopy Diva

◼◼◼◻ INTERMEDIATE +

Finished Size: 2¼" height x 15" circumference (5.5 cm x 38 cm).

SHOPPING LIST

Yarn (Medium Weight) MEDIUM 4
[3.5 ounces, 280 yards
(100 grams, 256 meters) per ball]:
☐ 1 ball

Crochet Hook
☐ Size F (3.75 mm)
   or size needed for gauge

Additional Supplies
☐ ⅛" (3 mm) Ribbon - 1 yard
   (1 meter)

GAUGE INFORMATION
5 sts = 1" (2.5 cm), 5 rows = 1" (2.5 cm)
Gauge Swatch: Crochet a 12 ch 8 rows
square swatch of scs to check your tension. Correct your tension if necessary
to make sure you have the right gauge
before you get started; you can change
hook size or yarn weight to correct your
tension and achieve the right gauge.

STITCH GUIDE
Loop Stitch
Our Loop Stitch consists of 2 rows. Row 1
the loops will be on other side of work,
Row 2 the loops will be moved towards
front side of work (see pages 42 and 43).

Collar Section
Ch 61.
Row 1: Sc in 2nd ch from hook, sc in
each ch across, ch 1, turn, (60 sts).

Row 2: *Sc in next 2 sc, 2 sc in next sc;
rep from * across, sc in last 3 sc, ch 1,
turn, (79 sts).

Row 3: Sc in 1st sc, **Loop Stitch Row 1**
in each sc across (Loops will appear on
other side of work, the side with Loops
is the front side), end with sc in last sc,
ch 1, turn, (79 sts).

Row 4: Sc in 1st sc, ***Loop Stitch Row 2**
in next sc, move loop to the **front** of
work; rep from * across, end with sc in
last sc, ch 1, turn, (79 sts).

Row 5: Rep Row 3, (79 sts).

Row 6 - Increase Row: Sc in 1st sc, Loop
Stitch in next 2 sc, move each loop to
the **front**, *(sc, **Loop Stitch** in next sc),
Loop Stitch in next 3 sc; rep from *
across, end with (sc, **Loop Stitch** in nex
st), **Loop Stitch** in next 2 sc, sc in last sc
ch 1, turn, (98 sts).

Row 7: Rep Row 3, (98 sts).

Row 8: Rep Row 4, (98 sts).

Row 9: Rep Row 3, (98 sts). Do **not**
fasten off.

Edging
Row 1: Sc in 1st sc, *(sl st, ch 1) in next
sc; rep from * across, sc in last sc. Faster
off. Weave in ends.

Finishing
Cut 2 pieces of ribbon the desired
length, tie one piece to each side of
collar for closure. Block (see page 44).

Loop Stitch Row 1

back yarn strand

1 Wrap yarn over forefinger, insert hook in next st, yo reaching across and over first yarn strand to reach back yarn strand...

2 Pull both yarn strands through st (3 loops on hook),

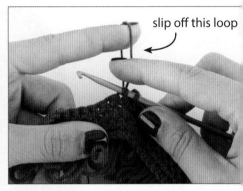

slip off this loop

3 Slip off the big loop on your forefinger...

4 And move [the big loop backward], hold in place between the thumb and index finger on your right hand...

5 Yo, draw through all 3 loops on hook to complete sc.

6 Completed sc. Front view Row 1. Start next Loop Stitch in next st.

Loop Stitch Row 2

back yarn strand

1 Wrap yarn over forefinger, insert hook in next st, yo reaching across and over first yarn strand to reach back yarn strand...

2 Pull both yarn strands through st (3 loops on hook),

slip off this loop

3 Slip off the big loop on your forefinger...

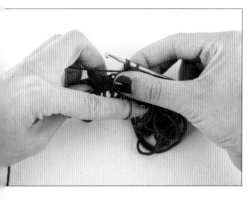

4 And move [the loop to the front of work], hold in place between the thumb and index finger on your right hand...

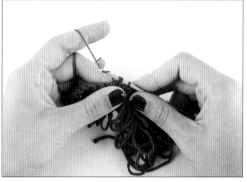

5 Yo, draw through all 3 loops on hook to complete sc.

6 Completed sc. Start next Loop Stitch in next st.

Front view Row 2.

Look for the camera
in our instructions & watch our
technique videos made just for you!
@ www.leisurearts.com/6379

Finishing Your Project

BLOCKING

Always check the yarn label for any special care instructions. Many natural fibers, such as cotton, linen, and wool, respond well to steam blocking. However, you shouldn't use steam or heat on mohair or angora. Many acrylics and some blends shouldn't be steam blocked at all because they will not "bounce" back to show the stitch definition again, and they can also melt!.

Use a hand towel or handkerchief and a padded ironing board. If you prefer, you can substitute a table or any flat surface that you have padded adequately.

Take the dampened towel or handkerchief, place it over the edge of the project, and steam with an iron, holding the iron slightly above the finished project. Lift the towel and repeat with another section all the way around. Leave the project in place until it is dry.

CROCHET INSTA-LESSONS

Holding your hook:
The best way to hold your crochet hook is like a pencil, with the hook tip facing you. Place your thumb on the grip 'flat' section of the hook. This gives you more control and freedom of movement.

The Secret is in your wrist!
It's all in the wrist. The hook doesn't move, let your wrist do all the work. Let your wrist bend and twist as needed. Your hook remains in the same steady grip...your wrist does the dance!

Tension, not too tight, not too loose, just right!
Your crochet projects will have a professional finish once you learn to master the tension. Just like a sewing machine has knobs to control the thread tension, your left hand is crucial to control the tension and feed the yarn smoothly to the hook.

If you hold on to the yarn too tight, your stitches will be small and tight, sometimes so tight that you won't be able to put your hook through the next stitch! If you hold the yarn too loose, your stitches will be "loopy" and big and it will be confusing to see where the next stitch should be worked.

Tension/Gauge matters

4 Steps to achieve the right tension or gauge
Gauge is simply measuring the number of stitches and rows per inch of crocheting. Our patterns will specify how many stitches or rows you should get per inch, gauge is usually tested on a single crochet swatch..
1. To achieve the right tension or gauge you must start with the yarn and hook size specified in the pattern, you can choose a different yarn as long as it's the same weight as your pattern.

Some yarns have the gauge on the packaging, for example, you might see a grid, with a 16 on one side and a 18 on the other side and a hook with a number by it, this is very helpful as it tells you that the average crocheter using the hook size they specified will crochet a swatch measuring the same as the grid on the label.

2. Crochet a swatch with the basic stitch specified in the pattern, usually is a 2" x 2" or 4" x 4" swatch made of single crochets.

3. Block the swatch (see left column) to help the yarn relax. Don't block acrylic yarns.

4. Place a ruler or a measuring tape across the center of swatch to see how many stitches "fit" in one inch. Do the same with the rows.

3 Things you can do to achieve the right tension or gauge Make adjustments if your swatch does not match the gauge for the pattern. **1.** Try changing hook sizes, either a bigger hook for bigger stitches or a smaller hook for smaller stitches. **2.** You may change yarn size and brand. **3.** Hold your yarn tighter or loosen your grip on the yarn to adjust the tension. Check your gauge periodically to make sure your garment will be the right size when you're finished.

Why Gauge is Important

You want to have your gauge be as close as possible to the gauge the designer used; this will ensure that your garment will turn out approximately the same size as the pattern indicates. Note that we said approximately because every one crochets with a different tension which will cause a slight variation in size.

It's important to check your gauge before you start a project and see how your crocheting compares to the gauge of the pattern.

Why Check Gauge?

Many crocheters think that working a swatch is a waste of time, however, you don't want to work forty hours on a garment that won't fit, that would be a bigger waste of time!

Gauge is important depending on the project, if you are making a scarf, a baby blanket, an afghan, flowers or a pillow, gauge might not matter much; but if you are working on a fitted project such as a hat or a garment, gauge makes a big difference.

One little stitch per inch more or less can make a big difference in the final size of your project. With a little math you can figure how one stitch can make your project a couple of inches bigger or smaller.

How to Make a Tassel

Cut a piece of cardboard the size of one of your credit cards, 2" x 3½" (5 cm x 9 cm).

1 Cut a piece of yarn 8 yards (7.5 meters) long and wrap around card lengthwise, you may use two different colors of yarn for each tassel (4 yards {3.5 meters} of each color).

2 Cut another piece of yarn 1 yard (1 meter) long and fold in half, slip through the middle of the wrapped yarn on one end of cardboard.

3 Tie a tight knot twice to hold tassel top together.

tie ends together with a knot

4 While holding the card, twist each group of strands at the top until they are tightly wound, make sure you twist each group in the same direction.

5 Pinch and hold both twisted ends together at the top and let go of the card, they will self twist together, tie ends together with a knot to secure in place and trim off uneven ends.

6 Slide tassel off the card and smooth down the loops.

wrap 5-6 times

7 Cut another piece of yarn 1 yard (1 meter) long and fold in half, wrap 5-6 times around tassel about ½" (12 mm) below the top, make sure you wrap it tight to keep tassel from becoming undone, tie a knot to secure in place.

8 Cut bottom loops and trim off bottom of tassel evenly.

9 Thread the remaining tails from Step 7 through a yarn needle and weave in down through the center of tassel. Block if necessary (see page 44).

How to Make a Pom-pom

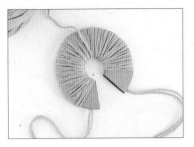 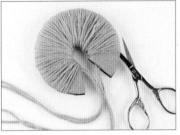  

1 Cut 2 cardboard circles using pom-pom template below. Cut a 36" (91.5 cm) piece of yarn, fold in half, and place between the two cardboard circles as shown above. Start wrapping yarn around the cardboard circles.

2 Wrap enough yarn around cardboard circles to make pom-pom thick and plump; with small sharp scissors, insert scissors between cardboard circles and cut yarn along the edge.

3 Cut along the edge being careful to keep pieces of yarn from falling off the cardboard.

4 Tie a double knot with the 36" (91.5 cm) strand, make sure it's very tight. Move strands around opposite side of first knot and tie another double knot.

 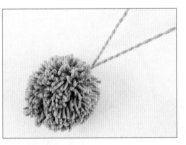 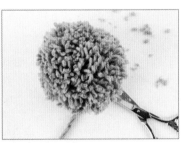 

5 Remove cardboard circles and fluff pom-pom.

6 Take both ties and twist each in the same direction, wind each end until twist is tight, pinch both ends together and let go pom-pom, both ends will self wind to form the cord. Tie ends with a knot.

7 Trim pom-pom all the way around to even all ends.

Completed Pom-pom
TIP: try using different colors of yarn on the same pom-pom for a fun look!

Running Stitch

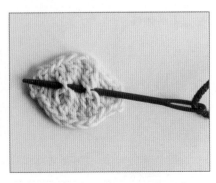

Running stitch is a basic embroidery stitch we use often to attach embellishments. It is made by passing the needle through and bringing it out again.

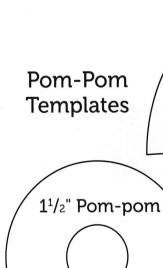

Pom-Pom Templates

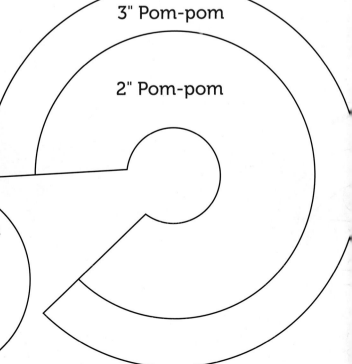

3" Pom-pom

2" Pom-pom

1¹/₂" Pom-pom

Stitch Guide

⊩ Magic Ring

A magic ring, also known as an adjustable ring or magic circle loop, is a starting technique for crocheting in rounds by creating a loop that allows you to put the stitches in; you can then draw the loop up tight to leave no visible hole in the center.

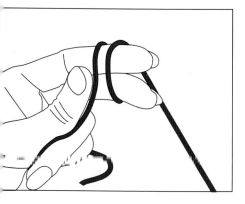

Leaving a 10" (25.5 cm) tail, wind the yarn from the yarn ball around your fingers as shown.

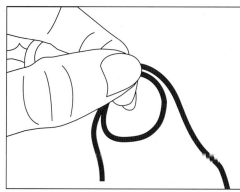

2 Grasp the yarn at the top where the strands overlap.

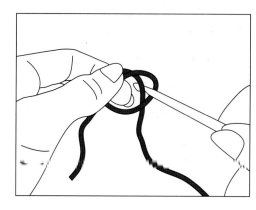

3 Insert the hook through the front of the ring and grab the yarn.

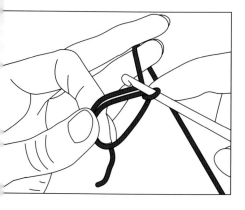

Pull up a loop.

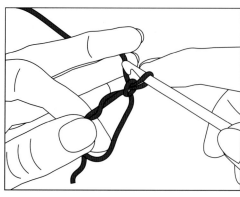

5 Chain 1; this chain is to "lock" the magic ring, it is not part of your stitch count. You may pull on the yarn to tighten the lock.

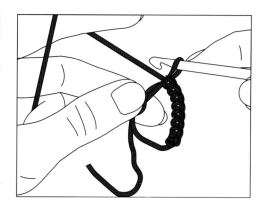

6 Chain 1, *insert hook through ring, yarn over, and pull through both loops on hook * (single crochet made) repeat from * to * to make as many single crochets as the pattern requires.

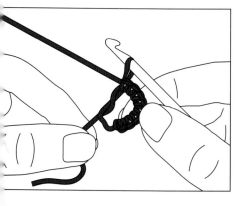

After completing the number of stitches the ring, grab the tail and pull firmly to close the ring.

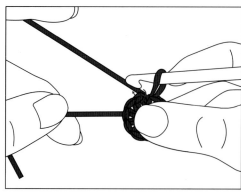

8 Join the ring with slip stitch by inserting hook through both loops of beginning single crochet (see pink arrow); don't insert hook through beginning "lock" stitch. Pull the tail again tightly to close center completely.

Stitch Guide

Holding the hook

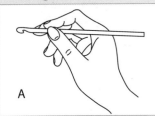

Holding the yarn

Slip knot

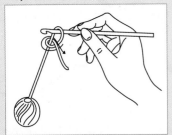

Start with a slip knot on your hook.

Yarn over (yo)

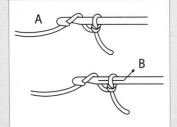

Yarn over (yo), pull through loop (lp) on hook.

Chain (ch)

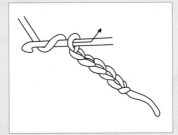

Yarn over (yo), pull through loop (lp) on hook.

Slip stitch (sl st)

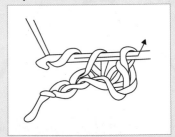

Insert hook in stitch (st), pull through both lps on hook.

Single crochet (sc)

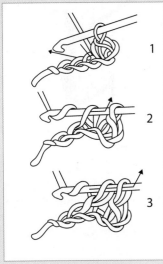

Insert hook in st, yo, pull through st, yo, pull through both lps on hook.

Half double crochet (hdc)

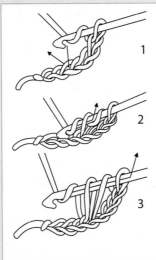

Yo, insert hook in st, yo, pull through st, yo, pull through all 3 lps on hook.

Double crochet (dc)

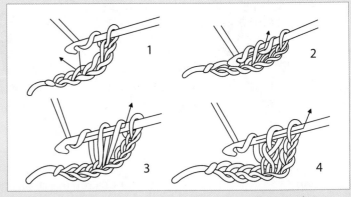

Yo, insert hook in st, yo, pull through st, [yo, pull through 2 lps] twice.

Treble crochet (tr)

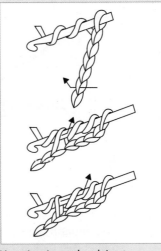

Yo twice, insert hook in st, yo, pull through st, [yo, pull through 2 lps] 3 times.

Double treble crochet (dtr)

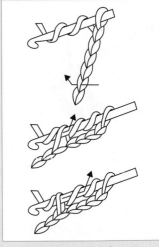

Yo 3 times, insert hook in st, yo, pull through st, [yo, pull through 2 lps] 4 times.

Front/back loop (front lp/back lp)

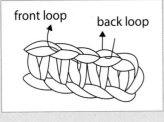

front loop   back loop

Changing colors

To change colors, drop the first color. With the second color, pull through last lp of st.